D0252767

An autographed limited edition of

URGENT,

UNHEARD STORIES

by

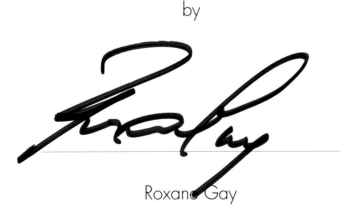

Roxane Gay

URGENT,

UNHEARD STORIES

BY ROXANE GAY

HARPER ● PERENNIAL

FIRST EDITION

ISBN 978-0-06-240661-3

15 16 17 18 LP 10 9 8 7 6 5 4 3 2 1

TABLE OF CONTENTS

TWO DAMN BOOKS:
HOW I GOT HERE AND
WHERE I WANT TO GO

I will admit, and I am not proud of this, I almost gave up—not on writing, but on the idea that I would find a publisher for my debut novel, *An Untamed State*. The manuscript had been making the rounds for some time, and the feedback was mostly positive but not positive enough in that frustrating way that makes you think, *If you think so highly of the writing, why don't you just buy the damn book?* Publishing is confusing.

My best friend talked me off the ledge time and again, sometimes gently, sometimes fiercely. She believed in my book when I nearly lost my faith. She had a gut feeling that the book would find a home, the right home. These days, she enjoys saying, "I was right all along." She is quite smug about it and I have to allow her this because, well, she was right all along.

Before I sold any books, I often found myself wishing I had an agent or a book deal. There was one small problem: I had not written a book, nor had I queried an agent. I was simply enamored with the idea of having a book with my name on it.

Slowly but surely, I got myself together. I assembled some of my writing about the Haitian diaspora experience and that became my first book, *Ayiti*. It was published by a micropress, Artistically Declined Press, run by a great guy with a lot of heart and passion for good books but no money to speak of. I signed the contract without an agent. I received no advance. I made my own e-book. My mother's wonderful photography graces the cover. *Ayiti* has remained in print for three years. I have earned $205.60 in royalties. That is a success story.

Of course I wanted more. I wanted the splashy publishing dream. I wanted a billboard in Times Square, wherein I wear a billowing vest while my book's title hovers nearby. I put together a short story collection, *Strange Gods*, which still hasn't sold lest you think it's all fun and games, and wrote a proposal for my novel. After a great deal of research and fretting, I queried one agent, in truth the only agent I have ever queried.

It's kind of absurd but she took me on, and once I wrote my novel, she tried to sell it for nearly a year. Then, my essays started getting some notice. Other agents began soliciting me, and though it was scary, and loyalty is important, I made a switch. My new agent was very confident, and before long she sold my novel and an essay collection, *Bad Feminist*, to two different publishers. It was surreal to get everything I wanted in one bright flash. It still feels surreal. People ask how I've gotten here and I hardly know what to say.

I had no idea what to expect when working with bigger publishers, though I'd heard the horror stories so I suppose I expected very little — no money for publicity, editors who don't edit, good books languishing without the publisher support they so very much need and deserve. I'm also a writer of color, and I was told my prospects as one were especially grim because publishers don't know how to market us and readers don't want to read our stories.

I did not know publishing moves glacially. When I eventually looked over each contract, I offered up thanks and praise for my agent. I know how to read, but I didn't understand much of what I saw in those papers. There were lots of arcane words and numbers, and basically I understood I would receive a rather modest sum of money in exchange for the publication of my books. The first and only dream dashed was the one where I could quit my job to write full time.

This next part may sound like a love letter but it is also the truth.

At Grove, my editor Amy Hundley championed my novel from the first day. Just after she bought the book, I was in Boston for a conference. She and her amazing partner came up just to meet me. I humiliated myself because that's how I roll. Two friends and I were at 826 Boston, where I would be reading that evening. There was a large Bigfoot statue. I was, as one does, taking pictures of these lovely friends licking Bigfoot's nipples. On the periphery, I noticed this woman but I didn't know who she was. I am awkward and don't engage with strangers well. When she said hi, I said hi kind of dismissively, and returned to my photo shoot because priorities. Later, during the reading, I realized that the woman looked familiar because I had stalked her on Facebook. It was a mortifying few steps when, during an intermission, I went to introduce myself to her properly.

The next evening, we went out for sushi and talked for hours. Amy wore fabulous glasses and sexy boots and she was gorgeous. I thought, *All my dreams are coming true because I have a chic New York editor!* She truly saw and felt what I was trying to do in *An Untamed State*. She loved Mireille, my protagonist, as much as I do. As Amy edited me, she only asked me to make the book better on the book's terms. She knew I didn't want to write around but instead preferred to stare directly into the violence. She supported that decision. She became a friend. Everyone else at Grove has been wonderful too. When I wasn't thrilled with the first cover design, they listened to my concerns. I ended up with French flaps and deckled edges and a beautiful cover. The sales team has championed the book. My publicist has championed the book and patiently read my crazy e-mails about travel arrangements. I am in the middle of a thirteen-city tour. A publisher could not do more to support a debut novel.

HarperCollins is publishing *Bad Feminist* in August. They are a much bigger publisher, a behemoth, and you can tell the difference—there are forms for everything, they have their own speaker's bureau, there is a bit of a procedure to get into the building. Though HarperCollins is a behemoth, people have been just as generous and available. Cal Morgan, who was long supportive of my writing, is always there with humor and generosity. He's fancy, but he also gets hands-on with writers. My editor Maya Ziv and I became fast friends because we enjoy very important television shows, romantic comedies, and music. She has a thick mane of red hair and is very New York chic as well. She talks fast and is always trying to get her authors' books in the hands of passionate readers.

When I visited the HarperCollins offices, there was a large phallic sculpture bearing the publisher's name in front of the building. I did a photo shoot, of course. The sculpture was really quite large, erect, and turgid. Inside the offices, everything was slick and hushed. On one floor, there was a video studio in which I filmed a video with a dapper woman who does something I can't remember. We had a sales meeting while sitting around a very big, shiny table. That table was so, so shiny. Everyone had clearly read my book and had great ideas for how to put it out into the world—buttons and T-shirts! Just outside of that meeting room was a huge Hollywood cutout for *Divergent*. It literally took up an entire wall.

9

This all sounds utopian. I have nothing to complain about. I have had fun. I have written exactly the books I wanted to write. I have learned a lot seeing how the proverbial sausage is made. Some illusions have been shattered (PCs dominate publishing instead of Macs), but my faith is mostly intact. Such a positive experience seems to be a rarity, so I am holding this blessing tightly in the warmth of my hand.

I still play devil's advocate with myself. There are so many books and talented writers out there. Nothing humbles you and clarifies your place in the writing world like obsessively refreshing your Amazon sales rank. This is, admittedly, a sad, sad thing to do, but I am not averse to suffering. Some days, there are literally 10,000 or 300,000 books selling better than mine. I stare at these numbers and whisper, "I am not a special snowflake."

There is also the reality of publishing: it is filled with people who love books, but there is always a bottom line. You are only as good as your last book. You vault over one hurdle and ten more appear. Are the reviews going to be good? Are there going to be reviews at all? Are you going to sell enough copies, in the right places, to the right people? Are you going to make the publisher's investment worthwhile? Anything could go wrong, I am constantly reminding myself. This past eighteen months could become a painfully glimmering memory of how good my writing career once was.

And then there is this. Professionally, my life has never been better and I am grateful for all of it. My personal life is a bit dismal. I have lovely friends and family who are endearingly supportive, but selling two books doesn't change my propensity for depression. Making a publishing breakthrough doesn't make everything better. I have all this good news and no one to share it with. I look at the growing stack of books I've written and I am so proud. I cannot help but think, *Writing is not everything. It can't be.*

The challenges of diversity in publishing are also on my mind, constantly. I wish I didn't have to think about these things, but I cannot overlook reality in the face of my good fortune. My editor Maya recently sent me an ad for *Bad Feminist* and several other Harper Perennial titles that will appear in magazines soon. It was a lovely ad, but I was the only person of color included. I e-mailed her and said, "This is nice but you could use more brown writers," and she said, "I know." She didn't make excuses, and we had a good conversation about diversity and publishing—it wasn't the first and it will not be the last.

I don't want to walk through the halls of one of the largest book publishers in the world and see no people of color in editorial positions. I don't want to look at bestseller lists, week after week, devoid of the excellent books being written by writers of color. I don't want publishing to perpetuate this atmosphere where writers of color and women writers worry that even if they get a shot, that shot won't be enough. In five years, I don't want to have the same damn conversations now that we're having about diversity in reading, writing, and publishing. I will, somehow, make sure more writers of color and women get the chance to be this lucky and hold such blessings in the warmth of their hands. I'm going to keep writing. I'm going to keep fighting. I've had a taste now of what publishing should be like for more of us. I am never going to stop.

THE TEN BEST BOOKS ABOUT MODERN VIRGINS

The virgin holds a mythical place in our culture. Virginity is a prize, something to cherish, protect, and/or conquer. In *Virgin: The Untouched History*, Hanne Blank notes, "Virginity is as distinctively human a notion as philanthropy. We invented it. We developed it. We disseminated the idea throughout our cultures, religions, legal systems, bodies of art, and works of scientific knowledge." Nowhere does this human notion flourish more than in literature.

From the New Testament of the Bible to Jane Austen's chaste women and the sultry sexuality of Nabokov's *Lolita*, we have seen writers grapple with the subject of virginity as it pertains to being unbroken, unclaimed, and unexplored. Even vampires get in on the act with the *Twilight* series, placing Bella's virginity at the sacrosanct center of the narrative. Or, put another way, you know virginity is a big deal when a vampire breaks a bed frame as he breaks his new wife's hymen.

Virginity is treated with far more grace and subtlety in Pamela Erens's latest novel, *The Virgins* (Tin House Books), a beautifully written story about two outcasts who form an all-consuming bond at an exclusive boarding school, as told, in secretive, sweaty detail, by a rather odious classmate. In fact, much of what is written about virgins is fueled by secretive, sweaty desire; the best modern novels on the subject—like the ten I've selected below—tell a story that, as in *The Virgins*, transcends the easiest or least of what we know about virginity. Such novels tackle the more complex question of what it means to surrender to a desire for the very first time. The attention is placed on the person in the virgin body rather than he or she who means to conquer that body, and sexuality becomes the beginning rather than the end of the story.

THE VIRGIN SUICIDES, BY JEFFREY EUGENIDES (1993)

In *The Virgin Suicides*, we know what's at stake from the outset, the title doing so much of the work of preparing us for the story to come. It is the seventies, and the Lisbon family boasts five daughters, ages thirteen through seventeen, who are budding with sexuality while their strict Catholic parents do everything they can to keep the girls cloistered at home, pure and, well, intact. This is also a story mediated through someone else's gaze—the boys of the neighborhood who covet the sisters and who can only watch helplessly as the young women succumb

14

to circumstance, their parents closing them off from the world ever more until, one by one, the Lisbon girls end their lives rather than remain subjected to an overly constrained existence.

FOREVER . . . , BY JUDY BLUME (1975)

Judy Blume is a foremost chronicler of adolescence and the ways it is fraught. When *Forever* was first published in 1975, it was groundbreaking in its frankness about sex, birth control, and young bodies and what they do together. In *Forever*, Michael and Katherine negotiate love and desire after meeting on New Year's Eve. Throughout the novel, the couple spends an inordinate amount of time discussing sex. Along the way, we learn Michael's penis is named Ralph, the most indelible of details. They are both young and naive enough to believe their love will last forever, and Blume makes us believe Michael and Katherine will overcome all the obstacles standing in the way of young love. At times, the book feels overly didactic, but given the time in which it was written, *Forever* strikes just the right note as a tender and true story about young sexuality.

ON THE ISLAND, BY TRACEY GARVIS GRAVES (2011)

Some books are just plain fun. *On the Island* is a May-December fairy tale—and the virgin here is a young man, T.J. When the novel begins, teenage T.J. is recovering from cancer and he has all the attitude of a young man

15

with a new lease on life. His family hires Anna, 31, to tutor T.J. while they summer in the Maldives, only their plane crashes and Anna and T.J. are stranded, alone, on a deserted island. Weeks become months become years. There are all sorts of calamities—sickness, personal hygiene challenges, a menacing shark, a tsunami. T.J. finally turns eighteen, and he and Anna give in to the growing attraction they've tried to keep at bay. They are, after all, fit and tan from island life. When Anna and T.J. finally get off the island (see what I did there?), the happiness they've found may not survive even though they have. T.J.'s virginity, though, has been taken well and thoroughly in hand.

THE LOVER, BY MARGUERITE DURAS (1984)

The prose in *The Lover*, by Marguerite Duras, is exquisite, lush, and deftly evocative of the time and place in which the novel is set. *The Lover* is the story of a complicated affair between a young French girl and her older Chinese lover in Indochina in 1929. Where most literary "first times" are rendered through cliché, Duras wields a fine touch: "And, weeping, he makes love. At first, pain. And then the pain is possessed in its turn, changed, slowly drawn away, borne toward pleasure, clasped to it. The sea, formless, simply beyond compare." The whole of this novel is beyond compare, and it offers a portrait of a young girl who is empowered rather than irrevocably harmed by her first, passionate love affair.

TOWELHEAD, BY ALICIA ERIAN (2005)

Jasira has been sent to live with her Lebanese father in Texas because her mother's boyfriend behaves inappropriately toward her. From the outset, this young girl, at the nascence of her sexuality, is a problem that must be solved, preferably from a distance. This is exacerbated when a neighbor begins to take advantage of Jasira in her Houston neighborhood, but *Towelhead* is not another sad, sad story. It is a coming-of-age tale about a young girl coming to terms with her body and what people want from it, and what control she can have over what happens to her. It's also about how young women can be failed by people with even the best of intentions, and how there is solace to be found in unexpected corners.

MAIDENHEAD, BY TAMARA FAITH BERGER (2012)

While vacationing with her family in Florida, Myra meets the intriguing Elijah. She wants something from him—to lose her virginity to him—but Myra returns home with her desire unfulfilled. She is surprised when, back home in Canada, Elijah shows up with Gayl, a woman who seemingly controls Elijah and, in turn, will control Myra herself. The three enter into an increasingly depraved relationship, marked by violence, pornography, and lust. *Maidenhead* is not simply a novel about virginity; it is a sharp examination of young female sexuality, race, and the ways people subject themselves to suffering and humiliation to get what they want. *Maidenhead* is a mani-

17

festo, as vivid as it is angry. *Maidenhead* is a reminder that stories about virginity can be nuanced and complex and about far more than unchartered territory.

INVISIBLE LIFE, BY E. LYNN HARRIS (1994)

E. Lynn Harris's *Invisible Life* was groundbreaking in exploring a black man's budding attraction to men. Raymond Winston Tyler Jr. is young, successful, and attractive. During his senior year in college, he falls into a relationship with Kelvin, a star football player, and has his first sexual experience with a man. Though their relationship is cut short, Raymond moves into his professional life in New York City, where he practices law and lives an invisible life, in the closet but wanting more. This book is often raw, but it does a fine job of exploring the complexities of race and class and sexuality in ways we rarely see in mainstream literature.

STORY OF O, BY PAULINE RÉAGE (1954)

Story of O is hypnotically erotic and terrifying in how quickly the book brings you into its world. In this slender novel, O is a young Parisian photographer ushered into the S/M lifestyle by her lover. Before long, she has become completely submissive, subsuming herself for her master's desires. It is the suffocating totality of O's submission that is so compelling. She gives herself over until there is nothing left to give, and still we are left believing O might give more. The transformation of O, from a virgin to kink into a full-fledged aficionado, is as stark as it is breathtaking.

CRASH, BY J. G. BALLARD (1973)

Sexuality and speculative fiction offer an interesting location for storytelling. *Crash* is a strange book about a new kind of sexuality, one where people are aroused by car crashes—ravaged metal, shattered glass, the destruction of the human body bloodied against leather seats. In the novel, James Ballard and his acolytes drive themselves further and further toward some manner of sexual satisfaction. As the narrator says in the novel, "I wanted to rub the human race in its own vomit, and force it to look in the mirror." This could stand, in many ways, for what always happens when we have sex—facing the most repulsive, most honest parts of ourselves.

"VIRGINS" IN BEFORE YOU SUFFOCATE YOUR OWN FOOL SELF, BY DANIELLE EVANS (2010)

All the stories in Danielle Evans's *Before You Suffocate Your Own Fool Self* are formidable, but the collection's first story, "Virgins," follows Erica, a young woman determined to lose her virginity, and in her quest to do so, she has sex with the wrong man. "Virgins" is about much more than that, but it primarily reveals how, even at a young age, our choices have consequences for which we may not be prepared, and how all too often, virginity is hardly about the woman to whom it belongs. Virginity is, unfortunately, what people make of it.

A LITERARY FLYOVER

Flavorwire recently released a slideshow of the hundred most important living writers in New York City ranked in no discernible way from Important to Importantest, which is now a word. We tend to love rankings, ferreting out the best of everything. If competition is possible in a given field, we will find a way to compete. That's the only reasonable explanation for the proliferation of competitive cooking shows.

There is a tendency to place the center of the writing universe in New York City. This is understandable—countless writers live there. Have you heard about this magical place called Brooklyn? The media certainly has. Most agents and publishers are based out of New York, where there are countless reading series and other trappings of the literati. There's a certain glamour to the city and what it means for writers. And yet. A little-known fact is that there are countless writers living in the rest of the country. The technical term for these writers is "college professors."

As I clicked through the Flavorwire list, I found myself in a vaguely delusional state, wondering if I might find my own name on the list. In doing this, I was ignoring two key facts: I am not an important writer, and I do not live in New York City, though people assume I do with surprising frequency. I live in a rural town—a rather charitable designation—in the middle of somewhere that is probably nowhere you know. There are no bookstores. I have to drive at least fifty miles to acquire my favorite yogurt—Cherry, Fage, 2%. The nearest major airport is 105 miles away. There are very few people of color. There's no black beauty salon, which is a real pain in the ass. There is very little to do, though, thankfully, there is a ten-screen movie theater in the middle of a cornfield. I call it the Corn Palace. I complain, often, about where I live because I don't like it here. I don't need to live in a city of The City, but I need more than this.

Still, there are benefits to not being in The City. This week, I went to the DMV to renew my car registration and there was no line. I walked right up to the counter, had a pleasant chat with the DMV lady, renewed my tags, and went on my way. My commute takes four minutes if I stop for coffee. I have this whole extra bedroom and my rent is still less than $1000 a month. This one time, at the gas station, a man on a horse pulled up to a gas pump. It was amazing. I still spend time thinking about what, exactly, he was doing. I travel once or twice a month so I get to join civilization with enough regularity

21

that I don't completely lose my mind. I also get to leave the chaos of cities behind. The last time I was in New York I had a blast. When my departing flight took off, I felt … relief save for leaving my friends (and I still cannot get over how many public bathrooms were so dirty except at WORD Brooklyn, where the bathroom was immaculate and pretty, as was the whole store).

At times I envy writers who live in the city, always going to book parties and benefits and other fancy events and knowing, seemingly, everything about everyone in publishing. Not being in the middle of that, however, and only joining in when I choose is a luxury. I live in the middle of nowhere, so there's no pressure to perform the role of writer. No one around me gives a fraction of a damn about the latest publishing deal or whatever we're all gossiping about on Twitter. I have time, enormous stretches of time, with very little to do but read and write. I'm not sure this is entirely healthy, but I get to actually be a writer with very little distraction. I try, though I don't always succeed, to not take such luxury for granted.

When these lists come out each year, highlighting important writers or important books or whatever else we would like to judge and rank arbitrarily based on subjective criteria, I cannot help but feel like we're being told a little of what we already know. The top three writers on the Flavorwire list are Philip Roth, Joan Didion, and Martin Amis.

These lists do matter even though when we don't like

what these lists say, we love to talk, exhaustively, about their irrelevance. If we're being honest with ourselves, these lists matter to the people who talk about them; they matter to those who are included or excluded. These lists matter because they reflect, for better or worse, what literary culture values and what literary culture seems to willfully ignore.

In thinking about the American writers I respect and enjoy most, many live in New York City, but many more live in other parts of the country. I would like to think that though they are all reasonably successful, they're not the names you would expect to see on these kinds of lists that tell us too much of what we already know.

In truth, I don't think about writers and their importance based on where they write. I focus on what they write, how they use language, the themes they're willing to explore, the ways they challenge me and my understanding of the world, how they make me feel and want and hope and love and hate. I'm thankful that can happen anywhere.

It would be impossible for me to create any kind of list structured around rankings, so I am calling what follows a literary flyover. A great sprawl, stretching from coast to coast, that focuses on writers who have made some impact on me this year (as well as those before it). What I appreciate most about this sprawl—and everyone will have a different sprawl, one that is always changing—is how it can reach all of us, no matter what city we call home.

Great writers! They are everywhere! I could do this all day! But for now, here is my sprawl.

East Coast Love

Outside of New York City, writers live throughout the rest of New York State. There's memoirist Daniel Nester (*How to Be Inappropriate*), short story writer Tina May Hall (*The Physics of Imaginary Objects*), and poet Aimee Nezhukumatathil (*Lucky Fish*), whose poems about identity and motherhood and the natural world are as intimate as they are intense.

In New Jersey, you'll find three-time novelist Tayari Jones, whose most recent novel, *Silver Sparrow*, continues to find critical acclaim. Claire Vaye Watkins is in Pennsylvania, and is the author of *Battleborn*, my favorite short story collection of 2012.

Elsewhere on the Eastern Seaboard there are writers like cultural historian Hanne Blank, who writes on really big, unwieldy topics in ways that respect both audience and subject matter (see: *Virgin* and *Straight* and *Big Big Love*, among others). There's also Dawn Tripp, who wrote a novel about a woman coming home, a fraught history between friends and an old mystery, and, best of all, Scrabble in *Game of Secrets*.

Up in Vermont, Megan Mayhew Bergman wrote another of the lovely short story collections I read in 2012, *Birds of a Lesser Paradise*, a book that reflected, in its structure, the ethos of each of the stories—that we're part of a complex ecology, and that the decisions we make have a profound effect on the systems we're a part of. She also has a warmhearted blog with lots of pretty pictures of Vermont.

In our nation's capital, you can find Danielle Evans, author of *Before You Suffocate Your Own Fool Self*, a book full of stories about women in complicated relationships, and broken men trying to find a former part of themselves, and how race and class shape what you can do with your body and what you can't, and how the ambition of young girls can force them into making decisions for which they can't possibly anticipate the consequences. Michael Kimball, who lives in Maryland, is the author of five novels, including the very moving *Dear Everybody*, which shows how much of a life can be remembered by what someone leaves behind.

SOUTHERN TREATS

The South is no stranger to great writers. There's Blake Butler, author of several books, including *Nothing*, the impossible-to-categorize *There Is No Year*, *Ever*, and *Scorch Atlas*, which has always impressed me with its visceral treatments of the human body.

Mary Miller, author of one of my favorite short story collections ever, *Big World*, is down South, and so is novelist, critic, and essayist Kate Zambreno, who has a bold and unrelenting voice. Essayist John Jeremiah Sulli-

25

van lives in North Carolina, in Peyton's house, and either you know what that means or you don't, and if you don't, if you aren't intimately familiar with the best television show ever, I hope you fix that.

Down in Florida, Jennine Capó Crucet is writing wonderful books like her story collection, *How to Leave Hialeah*, which explores the Cuban and Cuban-American experience with warmth and wit. Her stories are about love and the sticky heat of South Florida and race and family and what home looks like in the country you fled to or from.

MIDWEST MUST-READS

There's a great swath of country between the coasts. I don't know if you've been in the Midwest lately, but the literary scene there is really exciting and boasts more talented writers than I could possibly name. Lots of people like to pretend the arts don't exist there, but they would be wrong.

There is Lindsay Hunter, whose writing feels so damn real that the pages of her book, *Daddy's*, feel rough against your fingers. Alissa Nutting, author of *Unclean Jobs for Women and Girls*, can terrify you as much as she charms you with her stories. Not to mention Sara Levine (*Treasure Island!!!*), Alicia Erian (*The Brutal Language of Love*), Samantha Irby (*Meaty*), Cathy Day (*The Circus in Winter*), Benjamin Percy (*The Wilding*), and Kwame Dawes, author of more than twenty books of poetry.

In Michigan, you'll find Caitlin Horrocks, author of *This Is Not Your City*, a collection where each story reveals an innovative narrative style. She writes about displacement, and women who are somehow separated from what they want or need and how they suceed or fail to overcome that separation.

Here's also Matt Bell, author of the forthcoming *In the House Upon the Dirt Between the Lake and the Woods*. Bell is a meticulous writer, and you can see the care of his work in everything he publishes. His story "An Index of How Our Family Was Killed" is one I regularly read and teach because it is so formally interesting—an index that still tells a compelling, deeply emotional story.

In Ann Arbor is Elizabeth Ellen, author of *Fast Machine*, which contains an extensive volume of her creative output, including the essay "How I Stop Loving Dave Eggers and Stole Your MFA" and two of my favorite short stories, "The Last American Woman" and "Winter Haven, Florida, 1984."

TEXAS TWOSOME

There are great writers living in Texas, like Manuel Gonzales, who is writing the most fantastic stories. His debut collection, *The Miniature Wife: And Other Stories*, reflects the writer's towering imagination. The stories are written so believably, they handle the strange and surreal so carefully, that you want to believe the impossible is possible. Mat Johnson, author of *Pym*, and his razor-sharp wit are also down there.

27

WEST COAST SPECIALS

Out West, Shannon Cain is writing amazing short stories like the ones included in her collection, *The Necessity of Certain Behaviors*. Alan Heathcock is spending most of his time in Idaho, and in addition to writing one of the most celebrated books of 2011, *Volt*, he wins fancy awards and has opinions I share about bed-and-breakfasts.

In California, there is Randa Jarrar, author of *A Map of Home*, who just this week published a new, excellent short story, "Building Girls," about childhood friends finding each other once again, in unexpected ways. Lori Ostlund, author of *The Bigness of the World*, is also in the Golden State, as is fierce essayist and poet Saeed Jones. Susan Steinberg, whose forthcoming story collection, *Spectacle*, is a textbook on technical brilliance in prose, and Joshua Mohr, whose novel *Damascus* has one hell of an opening and is one part character study, one part evocation of place, also call California home.

Further north in Oregon, you'll find Lidia Yuknavitch, author of the searing memoir *The Chronology of Water*; Cheryl Strayed, whose wildly popular memoir, *Wild*, is a moving portrait of how a woman leads herself out of grief; and Todd Grimson, whose dark, witty writing in *Brand New Cherry Flavor* and *Stainless* are unforgettable. Then there are Pauls Toutonghi, whose *Evel Knievel Days* was another impressive novel released in 2012, and Elena Passarello, whose *Let Me Clear My Throat* is a smart and well-focused essay collection about voice and what the power of voice can do.

29

THE MODERN *LOLITA*: DRAMATIZING THE MIND OF A FEMALE PEDOPHILE IN ALISSA NUTTING'S *TAMPA*

Alissa Nutting's debut novel, *Tampa*, will give people something to talk about this summer and beyond. Though the novel's subject matter is controversial, Tampa is also impeccably written, full of smart cultural observations and no small amount of wit. *Tampa* is far bigger than the buzz, and more significant than the catchwords that will inevitably be attached to it.

Celeste Price is a sexy, attractive twenty-six-year-old eighth-grade teacher with a perfect body, married to a wealthy man who adores her. She drives a little red Corvette. She is living the dream, though there is a catch: she is a remorseless pedophile, intensely, obsessively attracted to fourteen-year-old boys. Celeste uses her classroom as her hunting ground, and in short order seduces young Jack Patrick, one of her students, using her intelligence and physical assets to keep him under her control. Her desires, though, offer diminishing returns because fourteen doesn't last forever and neither does twenty-six.

This is a novel about sexual deviance, relentlessness, and desire. It is compelling and disturbing, much like *Lolita*. Wrongs are committed, and flagrantly, but Nutting commits to her premise without wavering and demands the reader do so too. Over the past few weeks, I spoke with Nutting about her novel, what it means to transgress in literature, and how to walk the line between explicitness and vulgarity.

Are you nervous about this book in wide release, or am I projecting?

Yes … realizing I'm running low on dish soap is enough to give me a panic attack, so you can imagine what the publication of my explicit novel about a taboo-breaking sexual psychopath does to my heart rate. It's inevitable that the book will be misunderstood by many, and I know that will be hard. Writing transgressive literature opens you up to a double layer of criticism, because people are scrutinizing the subject matter as well as the actual writing. The target area for criticism becomes twice as large.

How do you define transgressive literature?

It's literature that protagonizes the unaccepted, whether through character or form or style.

I love the explicitness, particularly from a woman. When she uses her own vaginal juices to mark her classroom, I knew this novel was going to be great. How did you come up with the idea for Tampa, and how did you commit to the explicitness?

This type of story is so often fetishized in the popular media, and that got me thinking about the lack of novels whose protagonists are female predators, particularly sexual predators. There's a void there, and it's a conversation I felt compelled to start. I committed to the explicitness before I even began writing the book—in my mind, there was never a question of whether or not it was essential. If I was going to portray a dangerous character, I had to invest the text with the full amount of that danger or it wouldn't be a just representation. To be successful, I knew that the book had to make readers feel exceptionally uncomfortable. Otherwise I'd be whitewashing the topic.

Where do you see the line between explicitness and vulgarity? Do you like crossing that line?

These are really important terms in my mind. Sometimes I wonder if I actually believe in vulgarity, as a concept. Or I suppose I might believe in it too much—perhaps I have an exclusive belief in it! It seems to draw a divisive line between highbrow and lowbrow culture in a way that the term "explicitness" doesn't. Explicitness and vulgarity are both different subsets of honesty, both very necessary. In my own definition explicitness is more technical, vulgarity more creative, but both reveal something that mainstream culture likes to keep concealed. I don't think art can thrive in the absence of either one.

We rarely see fiction about women as sexual predators, in large part because we are faced with this dominant cultural narrative about dirty old men and their lecherous intentions toward teenage girls. Did you try to upend this narrative as you wrote *Tampa*?
Absolutely. I'd actually go so far as to say our culture has a really hard time casting females as sexual predators of male victims, even when the male is underage. If a thirteen-, fourteen-year-old boy sleeps with an adult female, there can be this narrative surrounding the act of it being a positive learning experience for him. That sort of attitude would never be applied toward a thirteen- or fourteen-year-old girl. Researching cases of female teachers who slept with male students, I was struck by how often there was even a construction of the female teacher as the victim—that the student pushed her into it, or instigated it, and she was somehow helpless against his advances, or vulnerable to them in a way that excuses her behavior. We have a really hard time breaking out of the male/aggressor, female/victim mind-set as a society. This book challenges that stereotype.

33

I felt a real empathy for Celeste. Reading of her exploits was horrifying and compelling, and still, I couldn't help but feel sorry for her and the futility of her desires. Where did this character come from and how did you get into her mind and body? Do you empathize with Celeste?

I wanted to meet a dangerous subject head-on with a dangerous character. Part of what makes Celeste so dangerous are the moments where you almost want to like her—where she makes you laugh, or where she addresses some aspect of being a woman in our culture that's easy to relate to or sympathize with, like how women are asked to constantly police their appearance and given the impossible task of maintaining a youthful appearance as we age. We're trained to root for the protagonist in a novel, and when we find that urge working against us or applied to a character's sinister actions, it's a challenging feeling. As a character, Celeste could've been far more sympathetic—she could feel guilt about what she's doing, or show concern for her victims. But then she'd lose a lot of her satirical power. The essence of Celeste is that she's a taboo and remorseless libido in high heels; the wizard behind the curtain with more humanity is the reader, not Celeste.

There is a sadness at the end of the novel when Celeste reflects, "For now, my youth and looks make this easy. I try not to think about the cold years ahead,

when time will slowly poach my youth and my body will begin its untoward changes. I'll have to pare down to certain types: the motherless boys, or those so sexually ravenous they don't mind my used condition." Even though the reason Celeste has this lamentation is repugnant, there's a lot more going on here. We live in a culture where youth and beauty are valuable currencies. Celeste is, as you note, vigilant about her appearance to remain attractive to young boys, but most women share in her vigilance for one reason or another. I'm not sure I have a question here, but I marvel at how this novel resides in such a specific location and still speaks to so much more.

It's an important aspect of this novel. Celeste is a female monster native to our current society. She's able to get away with having horrific actions and internal values because she's so good at excelling at the external values of youth and beauty that our culture champions for women. She worries far more about wrinkles than she does about going to jail, and for good reason: despite her actions, wrinkles are a bigger, truer threat to her than jail is.

The comparisons to Nabokov will be inevitable. Did you draw inspiration from *Lolita*? What else informed your writing of *Tampa*?

What I learned from *Lolita* is that it helps to make morally repugnant characters funny. Works of satire were very important to me as well—I'd actually say that narcissistic

Emma Rouault in *Madame Bovary* was a big inspiration in some ways. I also tried to examine and home in on the more charming facets of some of Edgar Allan Poe's witty criminal characters from his great short stories—characters doing awful things I couldn't stop reading about, basically. And of course I researched a lot of real-life cases where female teachers were charged with statutory rape or other illegal sexual acts committed upon underage male students.

How did you settle on the title of this novel?

I felt like it nicely represented the dualism of her character. With the text being so overtly sexual and boisterous on the inside, it seemed appropriate to title the book something ambiguously general—it mirrors the way Celeste represents herself as a harmless beauty with mass appeal when she's actually a complete monster.

Literary people are always looking for the "plug" and I've seen many a mention of your book as the most controversial book of the summer. That's sexy and all, and will definitely get more readers in front of the book. Is *Tampa* controversial? How do you feel about the way the book is being framed? What the hell does it mean for a book to be controversial, anyway?

I don't mind that title, particularly since there are a lot of snappy marketing headlines this novel is definitely not eligible for, like "Feel-Good Book of the Summer!" I don't know if my view of controversy is perhaps a little warmer and most positive than most or not; maybe it's too simplistic. I tend to think of it as anything that fosters debate, and to me debate is very healthy—controversy kind of requires the sunlight of democracy in order to grow, right?

I read your essay in the *New York Times* about going off of anxiety meds while you were pregnant. And though you used humor, there was a lot of vulnerability there. I actually see a lot of vulnerability in your fiction, both long and short. What does it take for you to make yourself vulnerable as a writer? How, if at all, do you put yourself into your fiction?

I've always been drawn to unfiltered characters in literature—it's such an interesting, privileged space to me to be able to get inside another person's head and see what they hide from others and what they show. Society as we know it is built upon repression and understanding what to conceal in any given situation. What you can't say to your boss is different than what you can't say to your grandma, which is different than what you can't say to your best friend, etc. But in literature that veil can be lifted completely—you hear what a character says to her boss, and you also read what she's actually thinking. That breakdown of dualism, that honesty, is so important and revelatory. When I write nonfiction I demand the same thing of myself as I do of my characters—I confess what's usually left unsaid in order to show a deeper, more intimate picture. To be more true and less composed.

Let's talk about the velour cover. Did you just die when you saw and felt it?

I did. I feel like it's a little necessary. It's a security blanket. When the book gets too scary, you can close it and pet the cover until you're brave enough to open it and start reading again.

What do you like most about your writing?

The humor. Tragedy would be incomplete without irony, in my view. I always include it.

A CONVERSATION WITH KIESE LAYMON

I first encountered Kiese Laymon's writing when I read "How to Slowly Kill Yourself and Others in America: A Remembrance." I was stunned into stillness. For a long while I simply sat with Laymon's words and tried to absorb what he had done. Then I reread the essay and was stunned into stillness again. I'm not going to lie. I was jealous—straight-up, green-eyed, how-can-some-one-write-this-damn-well jealous. That passed quickly, though, because Laymon's writing was too important and too necessary for me to be trifling.

Laymon's writing has reminded me that I read to better know the world and how it shapes us. As I've gotten to know Laymon's work through his essays, collected in a book also titled *How to Slowly Kill Yourself and Others in America*, and his debut novel, *Long Division*, I've been better able to appreciate how complex and varied the black experience in America can be.

His fiction, in particular, thrills me. *Long Division* is

an ambitious novel, and though it is raw and flawed, it is the most exciting book I've read all year. There's nothing like it, both in terms of the scope of what the book tackles and the writing's Afro Surrealist energy. There's time travel and a story within the story. From the first page to the last, something bigger than the story is happening.

Long Division is, in its gutsy heart, a novel about how a young black boy grapples with coming into manhood in the South. I knew I would love this book from the first chapter when Citoyen "City" Coldson is competing against LaVander Peeler in a "Can You Use That Word in a Sentence" competition: "The Can You Use That Word in a Sentence contest was started in the spring of 2006 after states in the Deep South, Midwest, and Southwest complained that the Scripps Spelling Bee was geographically biased." The novel is full of such seductively clever bits.

And then City is trying to explain the word "nigga." He explains to his friend MyMy: "Damn, girl. Didn't I just tell you not to say that word? Look. I know that I'm a nigga. I mean … I know I'm black … but 'nigga' means below human to some folks and it means superhuman to some other folks. Do you even know what I'm saying? And sometimes it means both to the same person at different times. And, I don't know. I think 'nigga' can be like the word 'bad.' You know how bad mean a lot of things? And sometimes, 'bad' means 'super good.' Well, sometimes being called a 'nigga' by another person who gets treated like a 'nigga' is one of the top seven or eight feelings in the world. And other times, it's in the top two or three worst feelings. Or, maybe … shoot. I don't know. I couldn't even use the word in a sentence, MyMy. Ask someone else. Shoot. I don't even know."

In one exchange, Laymon captures the fraught nuance of the N-word and its implications, in ways that are organic to the fictional world he is creating. The prose consistently offers incisive commentary, intriguing storytelling, and so much promise for Laymon's future work. Laymon and I recently talked, via e-mail, about race, his writing, and what words can make possible.

Is blackness a burden? If so, how do we carry it without breaking our backs?

Blackness, in and of itself, isn't a burden at all. In this nation, we all carry the immense burden of being human, but our backs are sore as hell because white Americans have failed to compassionately reckon with the worst of white folks. They tried to destroy us intellectually, psychologically, emotionally, economically, and we helped them out quite a bit. When people with more access to healthy choices and second chances obsessively want, and really need, you to have even less access to healthy choices and second chances, your back and your heart will tend to break. The wonder is that we're not broken. We're not broken. The wonder is that we're still here creating, still willing ourselves into generative kinds of human beings even though we're really, really, really, tired.

You wrote about how your mother raised you never to forget you were born on parole. How are young black children supposed to thrive under such conditions? Do you try to answer such an impossible question in your writing?

I think you thrive partially through milking your senses and your imagination, and placing yourself within a larger community of tough sensitive workers. My mother conflated survival with joy. She wanted me to be happy if I simply survived. I get it. I really get it. When a nation is implicitly and explicitly intent on destroying you and your son, survival feels like a win. But fuck that. As all-consuming and destructive as white supremacy is, it won't win. When I read your stuff, for example, I see that white supremacy hasn't won. I guess I'm dumb, but I believe in us and I believe that even though the game is rigged, we can actually win with love, tenacity, compassion, community, and the will to fight and strategize when we have to. The alternative is death.

You write both fiction and nonfiction. Which is your first love?

My first love was fiction. My grandma would give me these notebooks she wanted me to take notes in while we were in church and Sunday school. Sometimes I'd write these stories about this hole in the ground across the road from her house. Most of the time, I'd write these stories that ended with the sexy deaconesses in church telling me how sexy I was for an eight-year-old. In eleventh grade, I fell in love with the essay.

There's a real elegance to *Long Division*, particularly in how you balance telling a story, with really incisive racial commentary. What did it take to achieve that balance?
It takes a devotion to character, place, and black American literary tradition. And lots and lots of revision.

In *Long Division*, the book moves back and forth through time and also is quite coy about genre. I really enjoyed that playfulness and the nod to Afro Surrealism. Why don't we see more of such work from black writers? Both Afro Futurism and Afro Surrealism seem ripe with opportunity for writers of color.
It's weird that we don't see it in literature. I wanna blame the publishers, but I'm not sure that's fair. I know that we see tons of Afro Surrealism in our music. Tons. Hip hop, for all the true and dishonest shit that people talk about it, is our most explicit example of Afro Surrealism and Afro Futurism. I mean, my favorite rapper and writer calls himself André 3000. He has works called *ATLiens*, *Stankonia*, *Aquemini*. We don't have to look far for popularized versions of Afro Surrealism, or Afro Futurism. We just need more writers willing to engage with our best storytellers, whether those storytellers are literary storytellers or not.

43

Though I enjoyed the book, I struggled with the end of *Long Division*. I wanted the book, as a whole, to deliver more fully on its immense promise. Were you happy with how *Long Division* turned out?

People who love the book tend to love the last few chapters, while a number of readers I trust, like you, have said that they wanted it to deliver more. I'm not sure that those readers who loved the book "get the ending," but I think they might understand some of what I'm trying to do at the end with metafiction, the idea of runaway characters, the consequences of being young, black, and Southern in a crazy-making nation filled with crazy-making characters and narratives. The ending literally is asking readers to reread the book and consider all the sentences, consider who's writing whom, consider all that led all these kids underground. At the end, we see the beginnings (maybe) of a community of young black kids sweating, crying, laughing, wondering, wandering, and creating under the ground in rural Mississippi. Together. It's pretty daring and I'm sure I could get it "closer to right" with a few more revisions.

Why do you think publishing, even in 2013, remains so resistant to welcoming new voices to the literary table?

Most mainstream publishers don't understand our work or our communities. But they understand clicks. So I think we're seeing a change in what folks are willing to publish recently because they see that a lot of shit that they don't understand is getting thousands and thousands of clicks.

The South figures heavily in both your fiction and nonfiction. What does it mean to represent the South in writing as a black man? What is the South to you?
I try hard as I can to never "represent" the South. I want to explore my South, honor my South, extend the traditions of my South, but I don't want to represent it, translate it, or synthesize it for folks unwilling to love or imagine our people. The South, generally, and Mississippi, specifically, is home. It's home. It's why I read, why I write, why I try to love, and why it's hard as hell to beat me. We have been and can be a model of transformation for the rest of the nation and world. But we gotta stop being so devoted to death and destruction.

Memory seems so critical to your writing. How do you preserve memory?
I preserve memory through writing. I have to write to remember, to reckon with my memories. I write a lot of hours every day because I'm not good enough not to. When I'm not remembering and reckoning, I'm a terrible person.

Who have been some of your influences, and how do you acknowledge those influences in your work?

Jesmyn Ward, Margaret Walker Alexander, Charlie Braxton, André 3000, Octavia Butler, James Baldwin, Eve Dunbar, Toni Cade Bambara, Imani Perry, the Brothers Writing to Live crew, hip hop journalism in the nineties, dream hampton, Hua Hsu, my mother, grandmother, auntie, students, and the part of me that wants to be one of the greatest literary workers ever are the only reasons I'm able to write a decent paragraph every now and then. That's just the truth. I write to these folks in everything I create and I hope they can see and feel their inspiration in my sentences.

Is it possible for you to write without race, in some way, shaping what you do?

I think it's possible for me to write without race shaping what I do because "shaping" is primarily a tool of revision, right? But it's impossible for race not to, in some way, mingle with my prose. That mingling should happen in a way that explores intersections of sexuality, gender, money, and geography. Race and sexuality and gender and class and geography and history are always ingredients in everything ever written. Most writers are too lame to accept this as absolute truth.

I don't think enough writers, and particularly writers of color, talk about ambition. Where do you want your writing to take you?

I want my writing to help create a community of writers

and workers committed to honesty and brilliance. I want my work to help people work on becoming better at loving themselves, their partners, their communities, their people. I want my writing to help me make a lot of money so I can continue to help out a lot of the poor-as-fuck folks who inspired me. I want to create some of the best paragraphs, chapters, sentences, and books in the history of the world. And then I want to go to sleep.

What do you like most about your writing?

Structurally, every now and then, I do some things that haven't really been done before like in *Long Division* and the essay "How to Slowly Kill Yourself and Others in America." I like that sometimes it's really unafraid of the truth. Mostly, I love that the work I've created since July 2012 is going to last long after I'm gone.

URGENT, UNHEARD STORIES

I gave a reading at Kansas State University last week, and during the Q & A session, a young woman asked how I feel about the label "black woman writer." I said, "Well, I am black and a woman and a writer, so I'm fine with that label." I understood what she was getting at, though. Women writers and writers of color don't really have the luxury of being known simply as writers. There's always a qualification.

Earlier this year, Wikipedia editors began moving women novelists from the American Novelists category to the American Women Novelists subcategory. It was a strange move and one that met, as you might expect, with a great deal of resistance. It felt like segregation. It was an infuriating qualification of where certain writers belong in the public sphere.

In my early twenties, when I was first coming into myself as a writer, I was adamantly a *writer*. I was not a black writer or a woman writer. I did not want to be pigeonholed or backed into a corner by certain labels.

I still don't. My first novel, out next year, is about a Haitian-American woman who is kidnapped in Port-au-Prince, but the three novels I'm currently working on are quite different. One is a YA novel about a transformative year in a girl's life. Another is magic realism, for lack of a better description, about a miner so tired of the darkness that he flies an air machine into the sun, shrouding the world in darkness. The third is about a woman who has an unbreakable bond with the daughter she was forced to bear as surrogate for her sister-in-law and how she schemes to get her child back.

Are these the novels of a writer or a black woman writer? Does it matter?

Labels are troubling, but we love them. We love categorizing and naming things. There is comfort in knowing where things stand, but it is uncomfortable to feel like you can only stand in one place. What the hell is a "writer of color," anyway? Sometimes these words feel like they mean so little. When I read, I don't think about a writer's identity. I lose myself in beautiful arrangements of words and ideas. I lose myself in story and verse. When we call for a more diverse literary conversation, we simply want to see more of an acknowledgment of the diversity of writers who are beautifully arranging words and ideas. We are many. We are everywhere.

I have, as of late, kept an eye on the Penguin imprint Riverhead's list. In the past few years, they've published Danielle Evans, Najla Said, Mohsin Hamid, Khaled

Hosseini, James McBride, Catherine Chung, Dina Nayeri, and many others. When I asked Riverhead how they create such a diverse list, director of publicity Jynne Dilling Martin said:

> I think the diversity on the Riverhead list comes out of our editorial team's genuine curiosity and hunger for great new stories. We aren't doing it "by the numbers" but responding to the electricity of new perspectives that aren't treading the same worn paths we've been reading for decades. And because our Riverhead list is so small—just about thirty books a year—our team approaches publishing each book in a curatorial and handcrafted way, so that our writers don't feel like representatives [of their nationality or ethnicity], but like individuals with a unique perspective and an urgent, unheard story to tell.

This attitude is refreshing. Rather than thinking about diversity as this vague yet complicated notion, I like the idea of looking for urgent, unheard stories. This fall, many such stories abound from writers of color.

In *Men We Reaped*, Jesmyn Ward chronicles the lives and deaths of five young men in her life, including her brother, Joshua Adam Dedeaux. *Men We Reaped* uses a powerful structure—chapters about Ward's childhood are interspersed with chapters about each of the five men Ward lost, beginning with Roger Eric Daniels III, who died in 2004, and ending with the passing of Joshua Adam Dedeaux in 2000. *Men We Reaped* is not merely a memoir of grief; this book reads like an open wound.

The words carry a furious sorrow about how race and rural poverty can conspire to limit young black lives. The writing is strongest when Ward recounts her childhood and what she knows of her parents—how they came together, how they fell apart. Of her mother, Ward writes, "She resented the strength she had to cultivate, the endurance demanded of women in the rural South." This demanded endurance of women in the rural South is one I would have liked to see more explicitly explored. So much of this memoir focuses, understandably, on the lives of young black men cut short, but not enough attention is given to the women who mourn the men they reaped. Though these women stand at the margins of this memoir, it is clear that their stories are as urgent and necessary as the men whose lives and deaths have been so finely chronicled.

The high-rise public housing projects of Chicago have long carried their own myths. In *High Rise Stories: Voices from Chicago Public Housing*, Audrey Petty, who grew up on Chicago's South Side during the 1980s, has edited and compiled the stories of twelve former residents of the demolished projects, torn down as part of a redevelopment project that has not been nearly as successful as was envisioned. The neglect of Chicago public housing has only continued. "Defunded by city, state, and federal governments over the course of the 1970s forward, high rise public housing was chronically neglected and mismanaged... . These problems were compounded by ongoing crises that occasionally made the national nightly news: rampant gang drug dealing, turf wars, and gun violence." This neglected, violence-ridden place is the one most people imagine when they think of the high-rise projects, but families, actual people, lived in those buildings. In this volume, we get to hear their stories. As a whole, the collection is gripping and nuanced and unexpectedly moving.

Dolores Wilson lived in Cabrini-Green for fifty-three years with her husband and children. Though there was violence ("Snipers were a problem for many years") there was also a vibrant community. Her husband coached basketball and baseball teams. There was a drum-and-bugle corps, and well-organized building councils that did their best to fight the violence and governmental neglect. Her family not only lived in Cabrini-Green; they thrived. Eddie Leman lived with his mother in Robert Taylor Homes. In his conversation with Petty, he talked about the dangerous elevators, and his having to keep up his home because his mother was a drug addict. He made it out of the projects and joined the marines. When he left the military, he started working in mental health, noting, "Living in Robert Taylor, you're under a lot of stress and you learn to adapt, but there are people you get to know who have their own difficulties and sometimes the pressure is too much… . By the time I started therapeutic work, I had pretty much run across mental illness already." Leman also worked as a sheriff, did well, but life has a way of getting in the way. He was involved in a theft in 2003 and was sentenced to seven years in prison. These days, Leman is in graduate school, working, raising a family, and all he wants is to live "anywhere I don't have to watch my back. It's been so long since I relaxed." Each of the twelve stories in *High Rise Stories* reveals the simplicity of what so many people want and are denied.

Milk & Filth, by Carmen Giménez Smith, is a sharp feminist manifesto by way of poetry collection. Or that's how I read it. We bring what we bring to the reading experience. In "Your Data is Political," Giménez Smith takes on the way we mediate our lives online: "Your presence rises from scavenging: pages and words and webs and signs. You've become a target but without the old spy store gadgets." These poems are political and personal in the same breath. She takes on motherhood and cultural expectations placed upon women and what we consume and how what we consume shapes us. These are not poems that try to make the reader comfortable. They are uniformly challenging, at times guttural in tone and always fiercely intelligent.

One of the great joys of reading is finding books that detail experiences not often seen in mainstream literature. *Fairytales for Lost Children*, by Diriye Osman, is a raw collection of short stories about the queer Somali experience. These are often stories about exile from family, from country, from sanity, from self. Osman works well within the fairy-tale tradition. He uses patois and slang and rhythmic cadence to tell these stories in the only language they can be told. Though the collection would benefit from a more rigorous edit, the power of these stories is undeniable.

It's hard to know what to say about *White Girls*, by Hilton Als. These essays defy categorization. They are unwieldy and meandering and as self-indulgent as they are intriguing. In the first, "Tristes Tropiques," Als ruminates on his significant relationships with men, and their relationships with men, and the performance of friendship and interracial and intraracial dynamics. Of his friendship with SL, he says, "In short, we were not your standard Negro story, or usual Negro story. We did not feel isolated because we were colored. We did not want to join the larger world through violence or manipulation. We were not interested in the sentimental tale that's attached itself to the Negro male body by now: the embodiment of isolation. We had each other, another kind of story worth telling." That might describe this entire collection— not your standard Negro story. Als not only looks inward. His essays discuss Truman Capote, Flannery O'Connor, Michael Jackson, and much more. As a whole, the book is an interrogation of blackness and white womanhood. The prose is both intelligent and inscrutable. The essay "GWTW" is a masterpiece. This was a book I hated as much as I loved it for the incisive cultural criticism that has made me question nearly everything.

Another exciting new essay collection is *Meaty*, by Samantha Irby. She is well known throughout Chicago as a blogger and comedian, so it would be easy to assume that the essays in *Meaty* are all for laughs. Do not make that assumption. Don't get me wrong, you will laugh. Irby is self-deprecating, nearly to a fault. The way she sees the world is enthralling. There is nothing Irby won't write about, from the frustrating effects of Crohn's disease to sex and dating and the awkwardness of having a human body in the presence of other human bodies. She writes about race but not in the way you might assume. What most impresses me about *Meaty* is not the humor or honesty but rather the undercurrent of sadness that runs through many of these essays and how well Irby controls that emotion. This is an unforgettable book, the kind where the author unapologetically bares her heart and asks you to hold it tenderly, with care.

For many black women, Terry McMillan has written the stories we need to hear. From *Waiting to Exhale* to *How Stella Got Her Groove Back*, McMillan has found just the right balance between writing about contemporary black women and telling a damn good story. In her latest and very charming novel, *Who Asked You?*, Betty Jean is taking care of her two grandsons in Los Angeles. Her husband, Lee David, is sick and needing full-time care. Her daughter, Trinetta, is trying to get out from under the influence of drug addiction. Her son Dexter is in prison. Her sisters are all up in her business. Her best friend, Tammy, has her own issues, and somehow, while dealing with all this, Betty Jean is also supposed to take care of herself. *Who Asked You?* is an unexpected character study. So much of Betty Jean's life is dictated by the compromises she has made. If one word could describe this book, it would be "yearning" because Betty Jean clearly wants so much for herself and the people she loves but her sense of obligation often keeps her from reaching for more. In the end, though, this novel offers hope that Betty Jean might someday get the simple things she wants and richly deserves.

The *New York Review of Books* has released a new edition of *The Bridge of Beyond*, by Simone Schwarz-Bart, with an introduction by Jamaica Kincaid. When it was first released, The Bridge of Beyond was a bestseller, and it is easy to understand why. Most striking about this book is how magical the story is, even at its darkest. *The Bridge of Beyond* is a lush and entrancing fable about history and family and love. It is, truly, a hallmark of Caribbean literature.

You should also keep an eye out for Daniel Alarcón's mysterious and well-crafted *At Night We Walk in Circles*. Paul Yoon's slender novel *Snow Hunters* is exquisitely written—the kind of book that makes you think, this is the work of a writer's writer. Tao Lin's *Taipei* is not what you might expect. There is a meditative quality to the novel that held my interest and forced me to set aside my preconceived notions. Nina McConigley's *Cowboys* and *East Indians* offers short stories that explore place and displacement and identity, and that are all quite wonderful. Gabby Bess is one of my favorite young writers. I blurbed her collection, *Alone With Other People*, so I am biased, but her book is intimate and intelligent. The poetry and prose capture what it means to be a young woman in this digital age.

In 2014, keep an eye out for *Part of the Family?*, by Sheila Bapat, which looks at the rising movement to secure labor protections for domestic workers. *The Book of Unknown Americans*, by Cristina Henríquez, follows a Panamanian-Mexican couple who move to the United States after their daughter's accident so she might recover in better circumstances, only to discover that nothing is nearly as easy as they imagined in their new home. *Queen Sugar*, by Natalie Baszile, is a vibrant debut novel where a woman inherits a sugarcane farm in Louisiana and moves there with her daughter to try her hand at making sugar and creating a new life. In *Boy, Snow, Bird*, Helen Oyeyemi once again uses myth and fairy tale to tell a clever, strange story about race and the secrets of our skin.

Amazing writing from all kinds of writers is all around us. But I keep thinking about that young woman in Manhattan, Kansas. What I also wanted to tell her is this: Don't worry about what to call yourself as a writer. Don't worry about what people will call you. Write urgent, unheard stories. Read urgent, unheard stories.

THE BOOKS THAT MADE
ME WHO I AM:
I AM THE PRODUCT
OF ENDLESS BOOKS.

Nearly every day, a friend or acquaintance tags me on Facebook, asking me to share a list of ten books that have influenced me. Nearly every day, I read such lists from the same circle of friends and acquaintances. I understand the tidy pleasures provided by such an exercise, but in truth, I am not merely influenced by books. I could not limit a list of important books to a number or a neatly organized list. The list, whatever it might look like, would always be changing because I too am always changing. I am not influenced by books. Instead, I am shaped by them. I am made of flesh and bone and blood. I am also made of books.

The sweetest, most wide-eyed parts of me are made from the *Little House on the Prairie* books, by Laura Ingalls Wilder. They were some of the first books I read, and as a young girl in Nebraska, I loved knowing there were interesting stories to be told about life on the plains. This is also where my imagination began to swell. I imagined making candy with snow and maple syrup. I could hear the timbre of Pa's voice as he teased Half-Pint. I envied Mary's grace under pressure. I loved Almanzo Wilder. I loved him fiercely, that country boy. When he began courting Laura, I imagined what it would be like to ride in his sleigh with him, my face chilled against the brisk winter air, the rest of me warmed beneath heavy blankets and the rushing blood of Almanzo next to me, the thrill of his hand in mine.

The sweetest, most wide-eyed parts of me are made from *Anne of Green Gables* and *Anne of Avonlea*, Lucy Maud Montgomery, and *Little Women*, Louisa May Alcott.

59

I was a shy girl, but when I read, I was adventurous. Books made me bolder. I read stories, the titles of which I can no longer remember, about young girls embarking on thrilling adventures on wagon trains and fending for themselves, panning for gold. *The Chronicles of Narnia* made me believe I could slip into a wardrobe and emerge in a completely different world. Madeleine L'Engle's *A Wrinkle in Time* helped me embrace my intelligence, showed me how I was not merely bound to this world, not at all. *Charlie and the Chocolate Factory* made me believe anything was possible if I allowed myself to believe.

With *Forever* and *Are You There God? It's Me, Mar-*

garet, Judy Blume held my hand as my body changed and my heart changed and I began to feel less like a girl and more like a young woman.

My yearning was stoked by *Sweet Valley High*. My yearning was stoked by the lives of Elizabeth and Jessica Wakefield, their seemingly perfect lives, how everyone loved them and wanted to be them. I was nothing like them, but I wanted to be them or I wanted to be in their golden circle. Through these stories, I understood, intimately, what it meant to be on the outside looking in, utterly unable to look away. I understood what it meant to be enthralled.

As I realized I would never be like those girls, I read *The Outsiders* and learned there was fierceness in not fitting in.

Boarding school intrigued me, so I read about *The Girls of Canby Hall*, all thirty-three books, and then I went to boarding school and it was nothing like *The Girls of Canby Hall*—but I was a girl from Nebraska, and Shelley Hyde, one of the main characters from the books, was a girl from Iowa. Even though I was a stranger in a strange land, something about boarding school was familiar. As has always been the case, I was not alone because I had so many stories making the inside of me.

Something terrible happened to me, so I began to read voraciously about terrible things that happened to other women. This is where I learned gratitude when I did not think it would be possible. This is how I taught myself to believe I was lucky. In *Perfect Victim*, a young woman is kidnapped by a couple and held prisoner in a box beneath a bed for seven years. What she endures is unfathomable. I took no pleasure in reading this book, but I found comfort in knowing our bodies and minds are built to endure. I read this book so often the spine is now white and softened, the pages yellowed with age and the ministrations of my tearstained fingers.

Something terrible happened, so I read Maya Angelou's *I Know Why the Caged Bird Sings*. I learned that there was strength inside me if I could just hold on, if I could just find my way to reach my strongest place. I learned how to write what I could not speak, and how even if I could not use my voice, it was still there, waiting, waiting, waiting.

Something terrible happened, and I needed a different way of being in my body. I read *Stone Butch Blues*, by Leslie Feinberg, and for a while, I was able to live in my own skin on my own terms. In the stories of *Macho Sluts*, by Pat Califia, I found swagger. I turned to ink and marked myself with a new skin. I was able to live in my own skin on my own terms.

Lo-li-ta. *Lolita*. Vladimir Nabokov. From a novel about a pedophile and his unnatural lust for a young girl, I stared down the ugliest parts of what people do to one another and saw the faint, unbearably compelling glimmer of humanity in that hideousness.

The sharpness of my tongue was keened by Edith Wharton and the wit of *The Age of Innocence* and *The House of Mirth*—novels about social graces and the burdens of class and caged hearts, how passion stifled only deepens.

I found irreverence and quiet anger and the ability to laugh at the unfairness of the world in *How to Make Love to a Negro Without Getting Tired*, by Dany Laferrière, a writer with whom I share Haitian blood.

The most romantic parts of my heart flourished among the pages of *Pride and Prejudice* and *A Room with a View*. Zora Neale Hurston opened mine own eyes through *Their Eyes Were Watching God*, showing me love in a voice unlike any I had ever known.

My understanding of desire rose out of *The Lover*, Marguerite Duras, lush and sensual prose, the words thickly wanton. I closed my eyes and wished for the narrator's prescient arrogance. I closed my eyes and lamented these lovers who could never truly be together, their impossible passion, sweaty bodies coming together in the salt and sweltering heat of Indochina. And in those words there was a line that has always, always stayed with me: "My memory of men is never lit up and illuminated like my memory of women." My reading and writing have long been illuminated by the stories of women. I carry these stories with me.

Or my desire rises out of the *Story of O*, by Pauline Réage, a novel about darkness and submission, of allowing yourself to be entirely subsumed by the want and will of another. In this book I learned how submission is terrifying and freeing, how submission allows you to be on the outside looking in on yourself until you lose yourself. The *Story of O* made me want to get lost in myself or someone else or both.

My empathy grew when I began to understand how vastly the world extended beyond what I thought I knew. I read *Once Were Warriors*, by Alan Duff—a novel about a Maori family in New Zealand struggling through violence and addiction and loving one another too hard. I read Rohinton Mistry's *A Fine Balance* and understood the resilience of even the most abandoned among us. I read *The House on Mango Street*, by Sandra Cisneros, and *The Women of Brewster Place*, by Gloria Naylor, and *Love Medicine*, by Louise Erdrich, and *Krik? Krak!*, by Edwidge Danticat, and *For Colored Girls Who Have Considered Suicide When The Rainbow Is Enuf*, by Ntozake Shange, and *Passing*, by Nella Larsen, and *Giovanni's Room*, by James Baldwin, and this is a list that could not possibly end.

My writing ambition was sharpened by Margaret Atwood, *The Handmaid's Tale*, an unapologetically political novel that reminds us of what it costs to be a woman in this world or the next. My ambition, that toward which I aspire to write, has long been guided by Toni Morrison, *Beloved*, and through her words, seeing how a novel can be mysterious and true, mythical and raw, how a novel can honor memory even when we want to look away or forget. My ambition has long been sharpened by Alice Walker, willing to tell the stories of black women without apology, willing to write politically without apology—*Possessing the Secret of Joy*, a haunting, gorgeous novel about female genital mutilation that keeps me transfixed and heartbroken and helpless each time I read it, because sometimes the only way to tell the truth is to tell a story.

Today my writing ambition, my heart, and my mind are expanded by my peers who are writing the books I read with breathless anticipation and envy: *Normally Special*, by xTx; *Silver Sparrow*, by Tayari Jones; *The Empathy Exams*, by Leslie Jamison; *Prelude to Bruise*, by Saeed Jones; *The Book of Unknown Americans*, by Cristina Henríquez; *Ugly Girls*, by Lindsay Hunter; *Love Me Back*, by Merritt Tierce; *Salsa Nocturna*, by Daniel José Older; *A Map of Home*, by Randa Jarrar; *Forgotten Country*, by Catherine Chung; *Birds of a Lesser Paradise*, by Megan Mayhew Bergman. I take in these stories and become more of myself.

In all these books and in so many more, I find the most essential parts of myself. I become more myself. I learn what to hold most necessary when using my voice. I learn and continue to learn how to use my voice.

I am made of flesh and bone and blood. I am made of books. A list could not contain me.